Table of Contents

INTRODUCTION 4

CHAPTER ONE 6

What Is Fatty Liver Disease? 6

What Is Responsible For Fatty Liver Disease? 8

What Are The Identifying Features And Symptoms? ... 12

What Are The Different Types Of Fatty Liver Disease? 14

    Nonalcoholic fatty liver disease (NAFLD) 14

    Nonalcoholic steatohepatitis (NASH) 15

    Acute fatty liver of pregnancy (AFLP) 16

    Alcoholic fatty liver disease (ALFD) 16

    Alcoholic steatohepatitis (ASH) 17

What Complications Can Fatty Liver Disease Lead To? 18

    Can NASH occur in children? 18

    Diagnosis 19

Physical Exam and Medical History 20

    Blood Tests 20

    Imaging Studies 21

    Liver Biopsy 21

Treatment 23

    Dietary Strategies for Getting Rid of Fatty Liver 24

    Lose Weight and Avoid Overeating If Overweight or Obese 25

    Cut Back on Carbs, Especially Refined Carbs............ 25

    Include Foods That Promote Loss of Liver Fat 27

    Exercise That Can Help Reduce Liver Fat 28

Supplements That May Improve Fatty Liver 30

    Milk Thistle.. 30

    Berberine 31

    Omega-3 Fatty Acids... 32

CHAPTER TWO 34

Fatty Liver Diet 34

    Apple Cider Vinegar "Detox" Drink.......................... 34

The Easiest, No-Fuss, Roasted Turkey Recipe 35

Delicious Vegetarian Butternut Squash Soup 38

Baked Zucchini Fries 41

Pulled Sweet Potato Sandwiches 43

Creamy Roasted Parsnip Soup 45

Healthy Nachos (grain, soy, dairy-free) 48

Broiled Ginger Salmon... 51

Fresh Corn Salsa (Chipotle Copycat)............................ 53

Springtime Asparagus Soup 54

Pecan Granola Bars 56

Mexican Fruit Salad 59

Quick, Budget-Friendly Homemade Oat Milk Recipe ... 61

Gluten-Free Meatless Meatballs 63

Vegetarian Sloppy Joes 67

No Bake Blueberry Energy Bites 69

Sesame Pork Tacos 70

No-Bake Chocolate Coconut Cashew Bars 73

Easy & Healthy Avocado Chicken Salad 76

Vegetarian Minestrone Soup 78

Watermelon, Pineapple, Turmeric Smoothie 79

Ginger Lemonade 81

CONCLUSION 83

INTRODUCTION

If you've always considered fatty liver disease to be an alcoholic's burden, you may want to think again. There are actually 2 types of fatty liver disease – alcohol-induced and non-alcoholic fatty liver disease (NAFLD). Around 30% of Asian adults suffer from one of the 2 forms, and a recent study done suggests that the rate in US could be even higher.

If you have the disease, it means you have too much fat in your liver, which makes it less efficient at flushing out toxins from the body. More seriously, the disease can lead to liver scarring and eventually liver failure which is irreversible, so being in the know about how to lower your risk is valuable information indeed. While excess alcohol obviously plays a role in you falling foul of alcohol-induced fatty liver disease, other bad lifestyle choices increase your risk of developing NAFLD.

While the exact cause is not clear, NAFLD is often diagnosed in people who are obese, lead a sedentary lifestyle and those who consume a highly processed foods diet. Patients with NAFLD also tend to have high blood pressure and high blood cholesterol levels.

The good news is you can adapt your diet to reduce your risks for both types of the disease. If you are overweight, you should target to lose at least 10% of your body weight by switching to a lower-calorie diet high in fresh vegetables, fruit and high-fibre plants, and by avoiding added sugar, salt, trans fat, refined carbohydrates and alcohol.

Easier said than done, we know, which is why we've put together this cookbook for you on foods that can help you reach your weight goals and combat a fatty liver.

CHAPTER ONE

The liver is a vital organ that performs many important roles. One of its most crucial functions is that of metabolism. The liver carries out metabolism of carbohydrates, fats and proteins. In other words, all the three macronutrients present in our diets are metabolized by this organ.

There can be a variety of afflictions of the liver, ranging from infection to malignancy. However, globally, one of the main causes of liver disease is the overconsumption of alcohol. Liver disease caused by alcohol develops gradually and progressively and leads to conditions such as fatty liver disease and liver cirrhosis. Beyond a certain point, alcohol damages the liver permanently.

What Is Fatty Liver Disease?

Normally, if you are healthy and your liver is healthy too, there may be no fat or only a small quantity of fat stored in the organ.

However, when the percentage of fat in the liver exceeds 5% of the organ's total weight, the person is considered to be suffering from fatty liver disease.

In medical terms, this condition is known as **hepatic steatosis**.

This can be the outcome of excessive alcohol consumption or it may be entirely unrelated to alcohol.

The former type is known as alcoholic fatty liver disease and the former is known as non-alcoholic fatty liver disease. The non-alcoholic form is often related to obesity or even pregnancy.

Up to a certain point, fatty liver disease is reversible. However, if the conditions responsible for it are not actively rectified, it tends to give rise to liver cirrhosis and eventually permanent liver damage. In fact, fatty liver disease is acknowledged as one of the primary causes of liver cirrhosis. In extreme cases, patients may even die.

Fatty liver (steatosis of the liver) is one of the most common reasons people have abnormal liver blood tests. The liver is very active in handling fat. It takes lipoproteins (fats) from the blood, reworks them, and secretes them in a different form. The liver also makes and burns fat. When the balance among these activities changes, fat droplets can accumulate in the liver.

What Is Responsible For Fatty Liver Disease?

The main problem that leads to this form of disease is excessive deposition of fat within the liver itself.

Fatty liver disease is often associated with excessive alcohol consumption.

Alcohol alters the way that the liver normally processes fat, forcing it to store more than the normal quantities of fat.

It does not only inflict alcoholics or those with a severe addiction to alcohol. Those who regularly consume large quantities of alcohol, whether or not they are actually addicted to it, are liable to develop this disorder.

Insufficient or imbalanced nutritional intake can also precipitate this condition. For instance, if your diet is rich in cholesterol, there is a greater risk of developing fatty liver disease. A diet poor in nutritional value can also lead to fatty liver disease.

The following conditions may also contribute:

- Heredity

- Existing liver disease

- Inflammation of the liver due to autoimmune activity
- Being middle aged
- High blood cholesterol level
- Being obese or underweight
- Being pregnant
- Smoking
- Sleep apnea
- Side-effect of certain medications
- Having hypertension
- Insulin resistance
- Suffering from type 2 diabetes
- Other endocrine disorders such as hypothyroidism and hypopituitarism
- Hepatitis C
- Having polycystic ovary syndrome
- Metabolic syndrome
- Malnutrition

- Starvation and rapid weight loss

The cause of non-alcoholic fatty liver disease is complex and not completely understood. The most important factors appear to be the presence of obesity and diabetes. It used to be thought that obesity was nothing more than the simple accumulation of fat in the body. Fat tissues were thought to be inert, that is, they served as simply storage sites for fat and had little activity or interactions with other tissues. We now know that fat tissue is very active metabolically and has interactions and effects on tissues throughout the body.

When large amounts of fat are present as they are in obesity, the fat becomes metabolically active (actually inflamed) and gives rise to the production of many hormones and proteins that are released into the blood and have effects on cells throughout the body. One of the many effects of these hormones and proteins is to promote insulin resistance in cells.

Insulin resistance is a state in which the cells of the body do not respond adequately to insulin, a hormone produced by the pancreas. Insulin is important because it is a major promoter of glucose (sugar) uptake from the blood by cells. At first, the pancreas compensates for the insensitivity to insulin by making and releasing more insulin, but eventually it can no longer produce sufficient quantities of insulin and, in fact, may begin to produce decreasing amounts. At this point, not enough sugar enters cells, and it begins to accumulate in the blood, a state known as diabetes. Although sugar in the blood is present in large amounts, the insensitivity to insulin prevents the cells from receiving enough sugar. Since sugar is an important source of energy for cells and allows them to carry out their specialized functions, the lack of sugar begins to alter the way in which the cells function.

In addition to releasing hormones and proteins, the fat cells also begin to release some of the fat that is being stored in them in the form of fatty acids. As a result, there is an increase in the blood levels of fatty acids. This is important because large amounts of certain types of fatty acids are toxic to cells.

The release of hormones, proteins, and fatty acids from fat cells affects cells throughout the body in different ways. Liver cells, like many other cells in the body, become insulin resistant, and their metabolic processes, including their handling of fat, become altered. The liver cells increase their uptake of fatty acids from the blood where fatty acids are in abundance. Within the liver cells, the fatty acids are changed into storage fat, and the fat accumulates. At the same time, the ability of the liver to dispose off or export the accumulated fat is reduced. In addition, the liver itself continues to produce fat and to receive fat from the diet. The result is that fat accumulates to an even greater extent.

What Are The Identifying Features And Symptoms?

Fatty liver disease is often asymptomatic. In other words there may be no noticeable external signs of disease. However, having excess fat in your liver can lead to inflammation in the organ and symptoms more often arise as a result of this process. Patients who do experience symptoms typically complain of the following problems:

- loss of appetite

- weight loss

- weakness

- fatigue
- Nose bleeds
- itchy skin
- yellow skin and eyes
- web-like clusters of blood vessels under your skin
- abdominal pain
- abdominal swelling
- swelling of your legs
- breast enlargement in men
- confusion

Cirrhosis is a potentially life-threatening condition.

What Are The Different Types Of Fatty Liver Disease?

There are two main types of fatty liver disease: nonalcoholic and alcoholic.

Nonalcoholic fatty liver disease (NAFLD) includes simple nonalcoholic fatty liver, nonalcoholic steatohepatitis (NASH), and acute fatty liver of pregnancy (AFLP).

Alcoholic fatty liver disease (AFLD) includes simple AFLD and alcoholic steatohepatitis (ASH).

Nonalcoholic fatty liver disease (NAFLD)

Nonalcoholic fatty liver disease (NAFLD) occurs when fat builds up in the liver of people who don't drink a lot of alcohol.

If you have excess fat in your liver and no history of heavy alcohol use, your doctor may diagnose you with NAFLD.

If there's no inflammation or other complications along with the build-up of fat, the condition is known as simple nonalcoholic fatty liver.

Non alcoholic fatty liver disease is characterized by increased accumulation of fat, especially triglycerides, in the liver cells. It is normal for the liver to contain some fat and by itself, this causes no symptoms. In some patients, the excess fat can cause inflammation called steatohepatitis (steato=fat+hepar=liver +itis=inflammation), although there is no relationship between the amount of fat present and the potential for inflammation.

Nonalcoholic steatohepatitis (NASH)

Nonalcoholic steatohepatitis (NASH) is a type of NAFLD. It occurs when a build-up of excess fat in the liver is accompanied by liver inflammation.

If you have excess fat in your liver, your liver is inflamed, and you have no history of heavy alcohol use, your doctor may diagnose you with NASH.

When left untreated, Steatohepatitis can lead to cirrhosis (fibrosis, scarring and hardening of the liver). There is also an association with liver cancer (hepatocellular carcinoma).

Acute fatty liver of pregnancy (AFLP)

Acute fatty liver of pregnancy (AFLP) is a rare but serious complication of pregnancy. The exact cause is unknown.

When AFLP develops, it usually appears in the third trimester of pregnancy. If left untreated, it poses serious health risks to the mother and growing baby.

If you're diagnosed with AFLP, your doctor will want to deliver your baby as soon as possible. You might need to receive follow-up care for several days after you give birth.

Your liver health will likely return to normal within a few weeks of giving birth.

Alcoholic fatty liver disease (ALFD)

Drinking a lot of alcohol damages the liver. When it's damaged, the liver can't break down fat properly. This can cause fat to build up, which is known as alcoholic fatty liver.

Alcoholic fatty liver disease (ALFD) is the earliest stage of alcohol-related liver disease.

If there's no inflammation or other complications along with the build-up of fat, the condition is known as simple alcoholic fatty liver.

Alcoholic steatohepatitis (ASH)

Alcoholic steatohepatitis (ASH) is a type of AFLD. It happens when a build-up of excess fat in the liver is accompanied by liver inflammation. This is also known as alcoholic hepatitis.

If you have excess fat in your liver, your liver is inflamed, and you drink a lot of alcohol, your doctor may diagnose you with ASH.

If it's not treated properly, ASH can cause scarring of your liver. Severe liver scarring is known as cirrhosis. It can lead to liver failure.

To treat alcoholic fatty liver, it's important to avoid alcohol. If you have alcoholism, or alcohol use disorder, your doctor may recommend counseling or other treatments.

What Complications Can Fatty Liver Disease Lead To?

Usually, the liver is able to renew itself by replacing damaged cells. However, if the damage continues to occur and if unhealthy habits have not been rectified, the organ develops scarring. This is known as fibrosis. As the scarring gets worse it is irreversible. This condition is known as liver cirrhosis. In extreme cases, liver cirrhosis can lead to further complications such as liver cancer and liver failure.

In pregnant women suffering from fatty liver disease, there is a risk of liver failure or kidney damage in the mother as well as the foetus.

Can NASH occur in children?

Since the current epidemic of obesity begins in childhood, it is not surprising to find that nonalcoholic fatty liver disease occurs in children. Only a few studies are available, but the estimated prevalence among children 2-19 years of age is approximately 10%, the prevalence increases with the degree of obesity, and there is progression to cirrhosis. Although there is concern about nonalcoholic fatty liver disease among children, there is not enough evidence of benefit of treatment, and, therefore, no general recommendation has been made to screen overweight and obese children for nonalcoholic fatty liver disease. It is recommended, however, that children with suspected nonalcoholic fatty liver disease in whom the diagnosis is not clear should have a liver biopsy. Children should not be started on any drug treatment for non-alcoholic fatty liver disease without a biopsy showing NASH. Although there have not been studies in children to support the recommendations, loss of weight and exercise are the recommended treatment for children with nonalcoholic fatty liver disease.

Diagnosis

Since a good number of patients tend to be asymptomatic, the condition is often detected incidentally. Usually, this happens when the liver appears abnormal upon conducting imaging tests. Earlier detection is associated with a greater likelihood of recovery. Based on an overview of your symptoms and dietary habits or medical history, your doctor may suspect fatty liver disease. In order to confirm the diagnosis, the following investigations may be required:

Physical Exam and Medical History

When concern exists for the presence of fatty liver disease, the health care practitioner will try to find the underlying cause and risk factors. Questions may be asked regarding alcohol consumption, medication use (both prescription and over-the-counter) and past medical history, especially concerning previous history of viral hepatitis (the most common are A, B, and C) and immunizations against infectious hepatitis. Screening for diabetes may be appropriate.

Physical examination may reveal an enlarged liver that can be palpated or felt in the abdomen below the right rib margin. Otherwise, it may require the development of cirrhosis to elicit abnormalities on physical examination. These may initially include jaundice or a yellowish tinge to the skin and eyes, muscle wasting, hair thinning, abnormal skin blood vessels called spider angiomata, and splenomegaly (enlarged spleen).

Blood Tests

Blood tests may be helpful as screening tests for liver inflammation, although liver function studies such as serum transaminases (AST, ALT) may be normal or elevated and not necessarily related to the severity of the liver disease. Other liver tests such as alkaline phosphatase and bilirubin are often normal. Serum ferritin (a measure of iron storage) may be abnormal. In patients with NAFLD and NASH, cholesterol levels including triglycerides are often elevated.

Imaging Studies

Ultrasound of the liver can reveal patterns suggestive of fatty infiltration of the liver. Computerized tomography (CT scan) and magnetic resonance imaging (MRI scan) are also useful in the evaluation of fatty liver.

Liver Biopsy

A liver biopsy is considered the best way to determine the severity of liver disease.

During a liver biopsy, a doctor will insert a needle into your liver and remove a piece of tissue for examination. They will give you a local anesthetic to lessen the pain.

This test can help determine if you have fatty liver disease, as well as liver scarring.

Other tests include:

- Lipid profile tests.

- Elastography.

If detected early enough, fatty liver disease can be successfully resolved. The most effective way to do this is to reverse unhealthy diet patterns and lifestyle habits.

In case the patient is accustomed to consuming alcohol in excessive quantities, he or she will need to be supported in the process of overcoming this habit.

This can be hard to do and counseling may be required. Support groups can aid in the process of overcoming alcoholism.

Losing weight is a sound approach for non-alcoholic fatty liver disease.

However, if the condition has progressed too far and the patient has developed severe liver cirrhosis or even liver failure, the best option may be to undergo surgery for a liver transplant.

Treatment

The treatment of fatty liver disease is to decrease the potential risk exposures to the liver. For those with alcoholic liver disease, abstaining from alcohol is a must. For those with NALFD or NASH, appropriate diet, weight loss, diabetes control, and cholesterol/triglyceride control are important both for treatment and to prevent progression of the disease from NAFLD to NASH, and from NASH to cirrhosis.

Patients with celiac disease who maintain a strict gluten free diet can reverse fat accumulation in the liver.

Cardiovascular exercise can help promote weight loss and weight training can increase muscle mass. This not only improves metabolism and promotes weight loss, but the increase in muscle mass helps to sensitize the cells to insulin and reduces insulin resistance.

The patient and doctor should work together to formulate a plan that involves lifestyle changes. A balanced diet, increased in physical activity and exercise, and medication if needed to control cholesterol and blood sugar levels, can minimize the risk factors that lead to fat infiltration of liver cells.

Though there is much research underway, presently there are no medications proven to be effective in fatty liver disease; however, medications to control and lower cholesterol and triglyceride levels can be used in association with diet and exercise.

Patients with fatty liver disease should be seen routinely in follow-up visits to their doctor in order to monitor their liver function and progression to more serious liver abnormalities. Since weight loss, diet, and physical activity are the most important tools in minimizing the risk of fatty liver disease, and are the most effective treatments, consultations with a dietician and a physical trainer may be appropriate.

Dietary Strategies for Getting Rid of Fatty Liver

There are several things you can do to get rid of fatty liver, including losing weight and cutting back on carbs. What's more, certain foods can help you lose liver fat.

Lose Weight and Avoid Overeating If Overweight or Obese

Weight loss is one of the best ways to reverse fatty liver if you are overweight or obese.

In fact, weight loss has been shown to promote loss of liver fat in adults with NAFLD, regardless of whether the weight loss was achieved by making dietary changes alone or in combination with weight loss surgery or exercise.

In a three-month study of overweight adults, reducing calorie intake by 500 calories per day led to an 8% loss of body weight, on average, and a significant decrease in fatty liver score.

What's more, it appears that the improvements in liver fat and insulin sensitivity may persist even if some of the weight is regained.

Cut Back on Carbs, Especially Refined Carbs

It may seem as though the most logical way to address fatty liver would be to cut back on dietary fat.

However, researchers report only about 16% of liver fat in people with NAFLD comes from dietary fat. Rather, most liver fat comes from fatty acids in their blood, and about 26% of liver fat is formed in a process called de novo lipogenesis (DNL).

During DNL, excess carbs are converted into fat. The rate at which DNL occurs increases with high intakes of fructose-rich foods and beverages.

In one study, obese adults who consumed a diet high in calories and refined carbs for three weeks experienced a 27% increase in liver fat, on average, even though their weight only increased by 2%.

Studies have shown that consuming diets low in refined carbs may help reverse NAFLD. These include low-carb, Mediterranean and low-glycemic index diets.

In one study, liver fat and insulin resistance decreased significantly more when people consumed a Mediterranean diet than when they consumed a low-fat, high-carb diet, even though weight loss was similar on both diets.

Although both Mediterranean and very low-carb diets have been shown to reduce liver fat on their own, one study that combined them showed very impressive results.

In this study, 14 obese men with NAFLD followed a Mediterranean ketogenic diet. After 12 weeks, 13 of the men experienced reductions in liver fat, including three who achieved complete resolution of fatty liver.

Include Foods That Promote Loss of Liver Fat

In addition to cutting back on carbs and avoiding excess calorie intake, there are certain foods and beverages that may be beneficial for fatty liver:

• Monounsaturated fats: Research suggests that eating foods high in monounsaturated fatty acids like olive oil, avocados and nuts may promote liver fat loss.

• Whey protein: Whey protein has been shown to reduce liver fat by up to 20% in obese women. In addition, it may help lower liver enzyme levels and provide other benefits in people with more advanced liver disease.

• Green tea: One study found that antioxidants in green tea called catechins helped decrease liver fat and inflammation in people with NAFLD.

- Soluble fiber: Some research suggests that consuming 10–14 grams of soluble fiber daily may help reduce liver fat, decrease liver enzyme levels and increase insulin sensitivity.

Exercise That Can Help Reduce Liver Fat

Physical activity can be an effective way to decrease liver fat.

Studies have shown that engaging in endurance exercise or resistance training several times a week can significantly reduce the amount of fat stored in liver cells, regardless of whether weight loss occurs.

In a four-week study, 18 obese adults with NAFLD who exercised for 30–60 minutes five days per week experienced a 10% decrease in liver fat, even though their body weight remained stable.

High-intensity interval training (HIIT) has also been shown to be beneficial for decreasing liver fat.

In a study of 28 people with type 2 diabetes, performing HIIT for 12 weeks led to an impressive 39% reduction in liver fat.

However, even lower-intensity exercise can be effective at targeting liver fat. According to a large Italian study, it appears that how much you exercise is most important.

In that study, 22 diabetics who worked out twice per week for 12 months had similar reductions in liver fat and abdominal fat, regardless of whether their exercise intensity was considered low-to-moderate or moderate-to-high.

Since working out regularly is important for reducing liver fat, choosing something you like doing and can stick with is your best strategy.

Supplements That May Improve Fatty Liver

Results from several studies suggest that certain vitamins, herbs and other supplements may help reduce liver fat and decrease the risk of liver disease progression.

However, in most cases, experts say that further research is required to confirm this.

In addition, it's important to speak with your doctor before taking any supplements, especially if you are taking medication.

Milk Thistle

Milk thistle, or silymarin, is an herb known for its liver-protecting effects.

Some studies have found that milk thistle, alone or in combination with vitamin E, may help reduce insulin resistance, inflammation and liver damage in people with NAFLD.

In a 90-day study of people with fatty liver, the group who took a silymarin-vitamin E supplement and followed a low-calorie diet experienced twice the reduction in liver size as the group who followed the diet without taking the supplement.

The dosages of milk thistle extract used in these studies were 250–376 mg per day.

However, although experts believe that milk thistle shows promise for use in NAFLD, they feel that more studies are needed to confirm its effectiveness for both short- and long-term use.

Berberine

Berberine is a plant compound that has been shown to significantly reduce blood sugar, insulin and cholesterol levels, along with other health markers. Several studies also suggest that it may benefit people with fatty liver.

In a 16-week study, 184 people with NAFLD reduced their calorie intake and exercised for at least 150 minutes per week. One group took berberine, one took an insulin-sensitizing drug and the other group took no supplement or medication.

Those taking 500 mg of berberine, three times per day at meals, experienced a 52% reduction in liver fat and greater improvements in insulin sensitivity and other health markers than the other groups. Researchers say that despite these encouraging results, further studies are needed to confirm berberine's effectiveness for NAFLD.

Omega-3 Fatty Acids

Omega-3 fatty acids have been credited with many health benefits. The long-chain omega-3s EPA and DHA are found in fatty fish, such as salmon, sardines, herring and mackerel.

Several studies have shown that taking omega-3s may improve liver health in adults and children with fatty liver. In a controlled study of 51 overweight children with NAFLD, the group who took DHA had a 53% reduction in liver fat, compared to 22% in the placebo group. The DHA group also lost more belly fat and fat around the heart.

Furthermore, in a study of 40 adults with fatty liver, 50% of those who took fish oil in addition to making dietary changes had reductions in liver fat, while 33% experienced a complete resolution of fatty liver. The dosages of omega-3 fatty acids used in these studies were 500–1,000 mg per day in children and 2–4 grams per day in adults.

Although all the studies above used fish oil, you can get the same benefits by consuming fish high in omega-3 fats several times a week. Importantly, these studies show that certain supplements appear to enhance the effects of lifestyle changes. Taking them without following a healthy diet and exercising regularly will likely have little effect on liver fat.

CHAPTER TWO

Fatty Liver Diet

Here are some recipes focused on correcting the fatty liver disease;

Apple Cider Vinegar "Detox" Drink

Sure, your body is capable of detoxifying itself, but if your systems aren't in top condition and performing sluggishly you might benefit from a little BOOST. While one of the most natural ways to help your body's detoxification process is to stop eating processed foods and instead transition to a diet rich in whole foods – think fresh fruits, vegetables, whole grains, and lean proteins – some people swear drinking apple cider vinegar based on their own positive experiences. Perhaps you might also share in those same beneficial effects like increased energy, decrease in fatigue, less colds, better sleep, and more.

Ingredients:

• 8 ounces of warm, filtered water

• 1 Tbsp raw apple cider vinegar (such as Bragg Organic Apple Cider vinegar)

- 1 Tbsp fresh-squeezed lemon juice
- 1/4 tsp ginger
- 1-2 Tbsp raw honey (or pure maple syrup)
- Dash cayenne pepper

Directions:

Mix all of the ingredients together and drink in the morning or before a meal.

The Easiest, No-Fuss, Roasted Turkey Recipe

No basting, no trussing, no burning – just a flavorful, juicy turkey every time!

This easy Thanksgiving turkey recipe works every time as long as you stick to the correct size of turkey (12 lbs). You'll need a covered roaster that will fit your turkey. Make sure the roaster you use has a well-fitting lid to keep the heat in. If your lid closes loosely, just cover the lid with heavy duty aluminum foil and crimp it around the edges where the pan meets the lid to seal it well.

Ingredients:

- 1 fresh 12 lb turkey (size is important here)
- Kosher salt
- Fresh ground black pepper
- 1 stick butter, softened
- 1 whole lemon, remove the zest then quarter the lemon
- 1 Tbsp fresh thyme, chopped (sage works well, too!)
- 1 vidalia onion, quartered
- 1 head of garlic, cut in half crosswise (no need to remove the skins)
- 2 stalks celery, cut in thirds to fit into turkey
- 2 cups boiling water

Directions:

1. Adjust your oven racks so that your covered roaster will fit and preheat the oven to 500 degrees F.

2. Remove turkey neck and giblets, rinse the turkey inside and out, then pat dry.

3. Sprinkle about 1 teaspoon salt and 1/2 teaspoon pepper in the inside of the turkey cavity and place the turkey breast side up into your covered roasting pan.

4. Combine butter, thyme (or sage), and lemon zest in a bowl.

5. Run your fingers between the turkey skin and breast meat to separate the skin slightly and make a pocket.

6. Using half of the butter mixture, insert it under the skin of each turkey breast in the pocket you created and spread it out to cover the breast meat.

7. Spread the other half of the butter mixture all over the outside skin of the turkey breasts and thighs then sprinkle with salt and pepper.

8. Insert the quartered lemon, onion, garlic, and celery into the cavity of the turkey.

9. Cover the roasting pan and put into the oven for one hour.

10. After one hour turn the oven off but DO NOT open the oven door! Leave the turkey in the oven

undisturbed until the oven cools completely – 4 to 6 hours.

11. Remove the turkey from the oven, it will still be hot. Carve and perhaps serve with some Make Ahead Maple Roasted Sweet Potatoes.

Delicious Vegetarian Butternut Squash Soup

Crock-pot, Instant Pot, or stove top – either way you'll love this delicious vegetarian butternut squash soup recipe!

Ingredients

- 2 cups vegetable stock

- 4 cloves garlic, minced

- 1 carrot, roughly chopped

- 1 Granny Smith apple, cored and roughly chopped

- 1 medium (about 3–4 lbs) butternut squash, peeled, seeded and diced

- 1 white onion, roughly chopped

- 1 sprig fresh sage or 1 tsp dried ground sage
- 1/2 tsp salt
- 1/4 tsp freshly-ground black pepper
- 1/8 tsp cayenne
- pinch of ground cinnamon
- pinch of ground nutmeg
- 1/2 cup canned (13.5 oz unsweetened) coconut milk

Directions:

Slow cooker instructions:

1. Add vegetable stock, garlic, carrot, apple, butternut squash, sage, onion, salt, pepper, cayenne, cinnamon and nutmeg to a small (4-quart) slow cooker or large (6-quart) slow cooker. Toss to combine.

2. Cook for 6-8 hours on low, or 3-4 hours on high, or until the squash is completely tender and mashes easily with a fork. Remove and discard the sage. Stir in the coconut milk.

3. Use an immersion blender to puree the soup until smooth. (Or you can transfer the soup in two batches into a traditional blender and puree until smooth, being extremely careful not to fill the blender too full with a hot liquid). Taste and season with additional salt, pepper and cayenne as needed.

4. Serve warm, topped with your desired garnishes.

Stovetop instructions

1. Add vegetable stock, garlic, carrot, apple, butternut squash, sage, onion, salt, pepper, cayenne, cinnamon and nutmeg a large stockpot. Toss to combine.

2. Cook on medium-high until the mixture reaches a simmer. Then cover, reduce heat to medium-low, and simmer for 20-30 minutes until the vegetables are all tender and mash easily with a fork.

3. Remove and discard the sage. Stir in the coconut milk.

4. Use an immersion blender to puree the soup until smooth. (Or you can transfer the soup in two

batches into a traditional blender and puree until smooth, being extremely careful not to fill the blender too full with a hot liquid.) Taste, and season with additional salt, pepper and cayenne as needed.

5. Serve warm, topped with your desired garnishes.

Notes

For extra flavor, I recommend sautéing the garlic and onion before adding the remaining ingredients. Just heat 1 tablespoon oil over medium-high heat. Add diced onion and sauté for 5 minutes, stirring occasionally, until tender. Then add minced garlic and sauté for 1-2 additional minutes until fragrant, stirring occasionally. Then add the remaining ingredients and continue on with the recipe.

Baked Zucchini Fries

The best crispy BAKED zucchini fries with just a few ingredients – no special tools and no need to fry!

Ingredients:

- 2 to 3 medium zucchini cut into fries

- 1/4 cup flour

- 1/4 tsp salt

- 1/4 tsp garlic powder

- 1/4 cup Vegan Parmesan cheese (optional)

- 1/2 cup milk (whatever kind you like)

- 1 cup Panko breadcrumbs

Directions:

1. Preheat oven to 425F.

2. Line a baking sheet with parchment paper.

3. In shallow bowl or pie plate mix together the flour, salt, garlic powder and optional Vegan Parmesan Cheese.

4. In another bowl pour your milk.

5. In another shallow bowl or pie plate add the bread crumbs.

6. Dip the zucchini into the flour mixture, then into the milk, then into the breadcrumbs and place the zucchini onto the lined baking sheet leaving space between each piece.

7. Bake 20 minutes or until desired crispiness. NOTE: For extra crispiness, you can finish in the broiler for approximately 2 minutes.

8. Serve with your favorite marinara, dairy-free ranch or tzatziki sauce.

Pulled Sweet Potato Sandwiches

A pulled barbecue sweet potato sandwich even carnivores love!

Ingredients:

- 1 large or 2 medium sweet potatoes shredded – approximately 2 1/2 cups

- 1 tsp olive oil

- 1/4 tsp salt

- 1/8 tsp pepper

- 1/2 cup of your favorite barbecue sauce

- Sandwich buns, toasted

- Cole slaw or pickled cucumbers (optional)

Cole slaw

- One 8.5 oz package of cole slaw (of course you can shred your own red and green cabbage)
- 2 Tbsp vinegar
- 1 tsp sugar
- Salt and pepper to taste

Pickled cucumbers:

- 1 medium seedless cucumber, thinly sliced
- 1 Tbsp vinegar
- 1 tsp sugar
- 2 tsp water
- Pinch of salt

Directions:

1. If you're making the coleslaw or pickled cucumbers, do this first so they have time to sit allowing the flavors to meld.

2. Heat a deep sauce pan over medium-high heat.

3. Once hot, add oil and shredded sweet potatoes, salt, and pepper tossing the potatoes to coat them evenly.

4. Cook the potatoes for 5 minutes, tossing them frequently until they are lightly browned. Do not overcook as the potatoes will become mushy.

5. Once browned add the barbecue sauce and reduce heat to low. Cook for 10-15 minutes stirring occasionally until cooked to al dente.

6. Serve the pulled sweet potato on the toasted bun with your choice of toppings.

For the coleslaw or pickled cucumbers

1. Mix all coleslaw or all pickled cucumber ingredients above and let sit until ready to serve on your pulled sweet potato sandwiches.

Creamy Roasted Parsnip Soup

A creamy, comforting vegetarian soup that is incredibly simple to make with just a few ingredients, including the under-appreciated parsnip!

Ingredients:

- 2 lbs parsnips, scrubbed and cut into 1/2 inch pieces (look for small parsnips which are more tender)
- 1/4 cup extra-virgin olive oil
- 1 tsp Kosher salt
- 1/2 tsp freshly ground pepper
- 1 medium Spanish onion, diced (or yellow onion if available)
- 1 stalk celery, diced
- 1 1/2 quarts reduced-sodium vegetable broth, or homemade
- 1 bay leaf

Directions:

1. Preheat oven to 425 degrees F.

2. Toss parsnips, 2 tablespoons olive oil, 1/2 teaspoon salt and 1/4 teaspoon pepper together on a baking sheet. Spread the parsnips out evenly

over the sheet and roast until tender and golden – about 30 minutes.

3. Once parsnips are tender, remove from the oven and set aside.

4. Heat the remaining olive oil in a large pot over medium-high heat. Add the onion, celery, 1/2 teaspoon salt and 1/4 teaspoon pepper and cook until the onion is translucent – about 5 minutes.

5. Stir in the vegetable broth, bay leaf and cooked parsnips and bring to a boil.

6. Once boiling, reduce the heat to medium-low, partially cover and simmer gently until the parsnips are very tender and fall apart easily – about 15 minutes.

7. Remove bay leaf and pour the soup into a blender, filling pitcher only halfway as hot liquid tends to expand in a blender. Hold down the lid of the blender with a folded kitchen towel, and carefully start the blender, using a few quick pulses to get the soup moving before leaving it on to puree. Alternately, you can use a stick blender and puree the soup right in the cooking pot. Puree in batches until smooth and pour into a clean pot.

8. Warm the soup over low heat stirring occasionally until hot – about 5 minutes. Add water if you prefer a thinner consistency. Taste and season with salt and pepper to your liking.

Healthy Nachos (grain, soy, dairy-free)

These nachos cover it all! They're liver friendly, healthy, full of veggies, delicious, and a great option for those with food restrictions.

Ingredients:

• Tacos

• 2 Tbsp olive oil

• 1 medium zucchini small diced

• 1 medium yellow onion small diced

• Taco seasoning (your favorite or use the recipe below)

• 2 tsp minced garlic

• 7-8 cherry tomatoes cut in half

• 10 mini sweet bell peppers stem removed, cut in half, scooped out

- 10 leaves endive
- 1 lb ground turkey
- 1 cup vegan mozzarella regular cheese (if preferred)
- 1 small avocado peeled, pit removed, diced
- 1 lime
- 1 small handful cilantro leaves
- Salsa (your favorite brand)
- Salt to taste
- Pepper to taste

Taco Seasoning

- 1 Tbsp ground cumin
- 1 Tbsp ground smoked paprika
- 1 Tbsp garlic powder
- 1 tsp ground allspice
- 1/4 tsp ground cinnamon

Directions:

1. In a cast iron pan, add the olive oil, zucchini, onion, taco seasoning, garlic, and cherry tomatoes. Season with salt and pepper and sauté until the onion turns translucent and the tomatoes break down. Add a couple tablespoons of water if needed to loosen the fond from the pan.

2. Add the ground turkey and cook on medium low heat until no more moisture remains in the pan.

3. On a pizza pan, spread out the peppers and endive evenly in one layer. Top with 1/2 cup of the vegan cheese.

4. Add the meat and vegetable mixture over the peppers and endive and top with the remaining cheese. Put under the broiler for 1-2 minutes, until the cheese just melts.

5. Mix the avocado with a squeeze of lime juice from the lime. Season with salt and toss together. Spread it on top of the nachos along with a few spoonfuls of your favorite salsa and the cilantro leaves. If you like, give another squeeze of lime juice evenly across the nachos.

Broiled Ginger Salmon

Not just for heart health, omega 3s may protect the liver. This liver friendly broiled salmon recipe makes it easy to add salmon to your meal routine.

Ingredients:

- 1 1/2 pound skinless salmon fillet about 1 1/4" thick (Alaska, wild-caught)
- 1/3 cup reduced-sodium soy sauce
- 2 Tbsp honey
- 2 Tbsp fresh orange juice
- 1 Tbsp grated fresh ginger (about a 1" piece)

Directions:

1. Make sesame cucumbers: Put the sesame seeds in a small dry skillet over medium heat. Cook, tossing, for 2 to 3 minutes, until toasted. Let cool. In a medium bowl, combine the cucumber, jalapeño, lemon juice, oil, and salt. Stir in dill and sesame seeds.

2. Put the whole salmon fillet in a large ziptop plastic bag. In a small bowl, combine the soy sauce, honey, orange juice, and ginger. Reserve 3 tablespoons of the mixture and set aside. Pour the remaining mixture over the salmon. Squeeze out the air and seal the bag. Refrigerate for 15 minutes to let marinate (flip the salmon over halfway through so both sides marinate evenly).

3. Preheat the broiler (with the oven rack about 4 inches from the top). Line a rimmed sheet pan with aluminum foil.

4. Place the salmon on the prepared pan and discard the marinade. Broil for about 5 minutes, or until the top of the salmon begins to char. Pull the pan out and spoon half of the reserved soy sauce mixture over the salmon. Broil for 1 minute, then add the remaining soy mixture and broil for 1 minute more. The top should be nice and charred but not burned.

5. You can check for doneness by inserting the tip of a paring knife into the thickest part of the salmon. If the salmon flakes easily but still has a slightly darker orange center (medium-rare to medium), then it's done. If not, or if you like your salmon cooked more, then broil 1 to 2 minutes

more. Cut into 4 pieces and serve with the sesame cucumbers.

Fresh Corn Salsa (Chipotle Copycat)

Try this quick and easy Fresh Corn Salsa Chipotle Copycat recipe to complement many different foods – on a burrito, on top of fish, stir it in chili...

Ingredients:

- 3 ears of fresh corn on the cob, shucked

- 2 tsp jalapeños, finely diced (seeds and membranes removed)

- 1/4 cup red onion, minced

- 1/4 cup fresh cilantro, finely chopped

- Juice from one lime

- 1/2 tsp sea salt

Directions:

1. Preheat grill to medium heat.

2. Cook the shucked corn on the preheated grill, turning occasionally, until the corn is tender and specks of black appear on the kernels – about 10 minutes. Set aside until cool.

3. Cut the corn kernels off the corn (here are three easy tips for cutting the kernels off the corn cobs) and put the corn into a bowl.

4. Add the remaining ingredients to the corn and stir until well combined.

Springtime Asparagus Soup

Celebrate springtime's finest vegetable in a soup packed with nutrient-rich asparagus!

Ingredients:

• 2 pounds thin asparagus, tough ends removed

• 6 cups vegetable stock

• 2 medium leeks finely chopped, white and light green parts

- 1 large onion, coarsely chopped
- 1 large potato, cubed
- 2 stalks of celery, cut into 1/2" pieces
- 4 Tbsp flour
- Salt & pepper to taste
- 1/4 tsp ground nutmeg

Directions:

1. Cut the asparagus tips off, finely chop and set aside. Cut the asparagus stalks into 1/2" pieces.

2. In a pot over medium heat, add 2 cups of vegetable stock, asparagus, leeks, onions, potatoes and celery. Cover and simmer until asparagus is tender, approximately 15 minutes.

3. Pour the soup into a blender or food processor, add flour and process until very smooth.

4. Pour the blended soup back into the pot and add the remaining vegetable stock, nutmeg and reserved asparagus tips. Add salt and pepper to taste.

5. Cover and simmer, stirring occasionally, for 4 minutes or until the tips are tender and bright green.

Pecan Granola Bars

Not just a crunchy snack, pecans have high levels of good fats supporting lower cholesterol levels – PLUS they taste great.

Ingredients:

- 1 1/4 cups pecan halves

- 2 cups quick-cooking oats

- 1 tsp ground cinnamon

- 1/2 tsp fine sea salt

- 1 cup homemade pecan butter or creamy almond butter or peanut butter

- 1/2 cup maple syrup or honey

- 1 1/2 tsp vanilla extract

Directions:

1. Line a 9-inch square baker with one strip of parchment paper, cut to fit neatly across the base. The parchment paper will make it easy for you to slice the bars later.

2. For maximum flavor, toast the pecans: In a medium skillet over medium heat, toast the pecans, stirring frequently (don't let them burn!), until they are nice and fragrant, about 4 to 7 minutes. Transfer them to a cutting board to cool. Set aside 16 of your prettiest pecan halves for garnish, then chop the rest. Set aside.

3. In a large mixing bowl, combine the oats, cinnamon, and salt, and stir to blend. Set aside.

4. If you have made pecan butter for this recipe*, add the maple syrup and vanilla to your food processor or blender and blend to combine. If not, in a 2-cup liquid measuring cup, measure out 1 cup nut butter. Top with ½ cup maple syrup, followed by the vanilla extract. Whisk until well blended. (If you must, you can gently warm the liquid mixture in the microwave or on the stovetop.)

5. Pour the liquid ingredients into the dry ingredients. Use a big spoon to mix them together

until the two are evenly combined and no dry oats remain. Add the chopped pecans and stir until they are evenly dispersed. The drier the mixture, the more firm the bars will be, so stir in extra oats if the mixture seems wet. Conversely, if you used a super thick nut butter, you might need to drizzle in another tablespoon of honey to help it all stick together.

6. Transfer the mixture to the prepared square baker. Use your spoon to arrange the mixture fairly evenly in the baker. Cover the bottom of a flat, round surface (like a short, sturdy drinking glass) with a strip of parchment paper (see photo) and pack the mixture down as firmly and evenly as possible. Press the reserved pecan halves into the surface to create 4 even rows and 4 even columns (see photo).

7. Cover the baker and refrigerate for at least one hour, or overnight. This gives the oats time to absorb moisture so the granola bars can set. When you're ready to slice, lift the bars out of the baker by grabbing both both ends of the parchment paper. Use a sharp chef's knife to slice the mixture into 4 even rows and 4 even columns (these "bars" stick together better in a square shape).

8. For portability, you can wrap individual bars in plastic wrap or parchment paper. Bars keep well for a couple of days at room temperature, but I recommend storing individually wrapped bars in a freezer-safe bag in the freezer for best flavor. They'll keep for several months in the freezer.

Mexican Fruit Salad

Simple. Healthy. Tasty. Three simple words to describe the bold taste of this Mexican Fruit Salad recipe that should adorn your summer dinner table.

Ingredients:

Dressing:

- 2 Tbsp honey (or maple syrup or agave nectar)

- 3 Tbsp lime juice

- 1/8 tsp salt

- 1/4-3/4 tsp ancho chili powder (use more or less to taste)

Salad

- 2 1/2 cups honeydew, diced (approx. 1/2 a melon)

- 3 cups watermelon, diced (approx. 1/2 a melon)

- 3 cups cantaloupe, diced (approx. 1 melon)

- 2 1/2 cups pineapple, diced (approx. 1 pineapple)

- 1 1/2 cups mangoes, diced (approx. 2 mangoes)

Directions:

1. DRESSING: In a small bowl, combine the honey, lime juice, salt and ancho chili powder to taste. Add additional sweetener if you want it to be sweeter or another pinch of salt if you want it to be a little saltier. Set aside.

2. ASSEMBLY: In a large bowl, combine the fruit until thoroughly mixed. Dress the salad with as much or as little of the dressing as you like. Add additional chili powder to taste if desired.

Notes

1. You can replace any/all of the fruit with what you like. I've used diced avocados, jicama, strawberries, blueberries, kiwis, and orange slices

in the past. The possibilities are endless with this fruit salad!

Quick, Budget-Friendly Homemade Oat Milk Recipe

Avoiding dairy milk? Can't drink nut-based milks? Soy milk makes you nervous? It's time to try this oat milk recipe!

What's so great about homemade oat milk?

• It's incredibly inexpensive to make compared to nut-based milks.

• It's fast! If you were to make your own nut-based milk it would take hours. Ran out of milk for a recipe? You can whip this up in about 5 minutes.

• Delicious in coffee and tea without curdling.

• A wonderful option for children and adults who avoid dairy but are also allergic to nuts.

• The oat pulp that is left after you make the milk can be added to smoothies and oatmeal, used in baked goods, or you can even dry it out in a low oven and blend it into a flour. Virtually no waste!

Ingredients:

- 1 cup gluten-free rolled oats

- 4 cups water (use less water for thicker, creamier milk!)

- 1 pinch salt

- 1-2 whole dates, pitted or 1 tbsp maple syrup (optional, for making sweetened milk)

- 1/2 tsp pure vanilla extract (optional, for making sweetened vanilla oat milk)

Directions:

1. Add oats, water, salt, and any additional ingredients to a high speed blender and blend until the mixture is well combined, about 45-seconds. (Avoid over-blending as it can make the milk slimy in texture.)

2. Pour the mixture through a sieve or over a large mixing bowl covered with cheesecloth or a very

thin, clean kitchen towel to strain the oats from the milk. Remove the oat pulp from whatever you are using to strain the mixture and strain the milk a second time.

3. Pour your milk into a sealed container and refrigerate up to 5 days. Before using, shake well. Aside from using it in coffee, tea, cereal, granola or smoothies, it can also be used in baked goods as well where milk is an ingredient. Avoid heating the milk separately though as it will cause the milk to become thick and gelatinous.

While oats are gluten-free they can be processed on the same machines as gluten-containing grains contaminating the oats with enough gluten to cause a reaction in those with celiac.

Gluten-Free Meatless Meatballs

Often when we think of comfort foods they involve meat of some kind. If you're looking to try some meatless options, these meatless meatballs should be at the top of that list.

Ingredients:

- 1 cup cooked and cooled quinoa

- 1 15-ounce can black beans (rinsed, drained, dried)
- 2 Tbsp water
- 3 cloves garlic, minced
- 1/2 cup diced shallot
- 1/4 tsp sea salt (plus more to taste)
- 2 1/2 tsp fresh oregano (or substitute half the amount in dried)
- 1/2 tsp red pepper flake (reduce for less heat)
- 1/2 tsp fennel seeds (optional)
- 1/2 cup vegan parmesan cheese (plus more for serving)
- 2 Tbsp tomato paste
- 3 Tbsp chopped fresh basil or parsley
- 1-2 Tbsp vegan worcestershire sauce(optional // adds depth of flavor)
- Your favorite marinara sauce (optional, for serving)

Directions:

1. If you haven't prepared your quinoa yet, do so now (make sure it's cooked and cooled completely before use). Prep/cook time does not include preparing quinoa.

2. Preheat oven to 350 degrees F (176 C). Add rinsed, dried black beans to a parchment-lined baking sheet. Bake for 15 minutes or until beans appear cracked and feel dry to the touch (see beans in food processor photo). Remove beans from the oven and then increase oven heat to 375 degrees F (190C).

3. Heat a large (oven-safe) skillet over medium heat. Once hot, add water (or oil), garlic, and shallot. Sauté for 2-3 minutes, or until slightly softened, stirring frequently. Remove from heat (and reserve pan for later use).

4. Add black beans to a food processor along with garlic, shallot, sea salt, oregano, red pepper flake, and fennel (optional) and pulse into a loose meal (DON'T overmix). Then add cooked/cooled quinoa, vegan parmesan cheese, tomato paste, fresh basil or parsley, and Worcestershire (optional). Pulse to combine until a textured dough forms (you're not looking for a purée, but it should be semi-tacky).

5. Taste and adjust flavor as needed, adding more salt for saltiness/depth of flavor, red pepper flake for heat, herbs for earthiness, or Worcestershire (optional) for more depth of flavor. If it's too tacky or wet, add more vegan parmesan cheese and pulse to combine (we added a bit more).

6. Scoop out heaping 1 1/2 Tbsp amounts (using this scoop or a Tablespoon) and gently form into small balls using your hands. Add to a plate and refrigerate for 15 minutes.

7. Heat an oven-safe metal or cast-iron skillet over medium heat. Once hot, add the meatballs and sauté for a few minutes, gently turning the meatballs to get a slight crust on either side. Then transfer to the oven and bake for 20-30 minutes or until golden brown on the edges and slightly dry to the touch.

8. These meatballs are delicious as is, or you can add some marinara to the pan and heat over medium heat for 5 minutes (or until bubbling / hot) to infuse more flavor.

9. Serve with marinara and additional vegan parmesan cheese (optional)! These are also delicious atop any pasta. Leftover meatballs keep for 4-5 days in the refrigerator or 1 month in the

freezer. Reheat in the microwave or in a 375-degree F (190 C) oven until warmed through.

Vegetarian Sloppy Joes

A childhood classic, made with tempeh instead of beef. For those with a fatty liver, eating soy protein may help alleviate some of the symptoms of fatty liver disease.

Ingredients:

- 2 Tbsp vegetable oil

- 1/2 large onion, minced

- 16 ounces packaged tempeh

- 1 green bell pepper, minced

- 2 cloves garlic, minced

- 1/2 cup tomato sauce

- 1 Tbsp vegan Worcestershire sauce

- 1 Tbsp honey

- 1 Tbsp blackstrap molasses

- 1/4 tsp cayenne pepper (optional)
- 1/4 tsp celery seed
- 1/4 tsp ground cumin
- 1/4 tsp salt
- 1/2 tsp ground coriander
- 1/2 tsp dried thyme
- 1/2 tsp oregano
- 1/2 tsp paprika
- 1 pinch ground black pepper
- Four lightly toasted hamburger buns

Directions:

1. Heat a large pan over medium heat, add oil and onion cooking until translucent, about 4-5 minutes.

2. Crumble the tempeh into the pan and cook, while stirring, until golden brown.

3. Once tempeh is golden, add the pepper and garlic, cooking another 2-3 minutes.

4. Stir in the remaining ingredients (except the buns) and simmer 10-15 minutes.

5. Spoon hot Sloppy Joe mixture onto the lightly toasted hamburger buns and serve.

Soy protein alleviates symptoms of fatty liver disease, study suggests – University of Illinois researchers have shown how soy protein could significantly reduce fat accumulation and triglycerides in the livers of obese patients by partially restoring the function of a key signaling pathway in the organ.

No Bake Blueberry Energy Bites

These quick, no bake treats are made with just a few delicious liver-friendly ingredients including antioxidant rich blueberries!

Ingredients:

- 2 cup raw old-fashioned oats

- 1/2 cup almond butter

- 1/2 cup honey

- 1 teaspoon alcohol-free vanilla

- 1/2 teaspoon cinnamon
- 1 cup dried blueberries

Directions:

1. In a large bowl, mix together oats, almond butter, honey, vanilla, and cinnamon.

2. Next fold in the blueberries until they are evenly distributed in the mix.

3. Refrigerate mixture for 30-60 minutes, or until it becomes solidified.

4. Mold mixture into bite-sized balls and serve. You can keep the energy bites in an air tight container in the refrigerator up to one week or freeze and defrost when needed.

Sesame Pork Tacos

If you need some healthy inspiration for your next Taco Tuesday, look no further. The quick pickled vegetables create a delicious Asian-inspired taco that is over the top!

Ingredients

- 1 cup thinly sliced English cucumber (seedless)
- 6 small radishes, thinly sliced
- 1/4 cup white wine vinegar
- 4 tsp sugar (divided in half)
- 2 tbsp olive oil (or cooking oil of your choice)
- 4 small scallions, white parts thinly sliced
- 1 cup shredded red cabbage
- 1 1/2 lbs ground pork
- 2 tsp garlic powder
- 2 tbsp sesame oil
- 2 tbsp soy sauce
- 2 tsp Sriracha (optional)
- 12 small tortillas
- 2 tsp fresh cilantro, chopped
- 1/2 cup sour cream
- Salt & pepper

Directions:

1. To a small bowl, add the cucumbers, radishes, vinegar, 2 teaspoons of sugar, and pinch of salt and pepper. Stir together and set aside for the flavors to combine.

2. Heat a large pan over medium-high heat and add oil.

3. Add the scallions and cabbage to the pan and cook until softened, about 4 minutes, stirring occasionally.

4. To the pan, add pork, garlic powder, and 2 teaspoons of sugar. Break the meat up into pieces as it cooks and cook for about 4 minutes, stirring occasionally (it will continue to cook after adding additional ingredients).

5. Add the sesame oil, soy sauce, Sriracha (optional), to the pan and stir to combine. Once liquid has reduced slightly, taste and add salt and pepper as needed.

6. Heat the tortillas by wrapping them in a damp paper towel and placing them in the microwave for 30 seconds.

7. Build your tacos: Spread a small amount of sour cream in the center of your tortilla, add your pork filling, a sprinkling of chopped cilantro and, using a slotted spoon, retrieve the pickled cucumbers and radishes and place on top of the meat mixture.

No-Bake Chocolate Coconut Cashew Bars

A delicious combination of healthy ingredients, no added sugar, and no baking. What's not to love!

Ingredients

- 1 1/4 cup dried unsulphured figs or about 5-6 ounces (stems cut off)

- 2 cups raw cashews

- 1 cup unsweetened coconut flakes (plus extra for topping)

- 1 tsp alcohol-free vanilla

- 1/4 tsp sea salt

- 1/3 to 2/3 cup or more of dark chocolate chips, to melt

- optional add-ins 1 tbsp protein powder, chia, nuts, cocoa powder.

Directions:

1. Line a square baking pan with parchment paper. Set aside.

2. Next make sure your dried figs have all the stems cut off.

3. Place cashew, coconut, salt, vanilla, and figs in food processor. (If you don't have a high powered food processor or blender, then divide the ingredients in half and blend/grind in two batches).

4. Blend until mixture is fine and able to stick together well. See pictures above.

5. Pour mixture into baking dish and press down well.

6. While the fig/cashew mix sets in pan, melt your dark chocolate.

7. Place dark chocolate in a microwave safe bowl or on stove top. Heat until melted. About 60-90 seconds in microwave mixing half way.

8. Next pour the chocolate over the cashew coconut batter and spread it evenly in the dish to cover all. Note: if you need more dark chocolate to cover, just melt an additional 1/4 cup.

9. Optional topping – Sprinkle extra coconut, cashew, sliced fig, and dash of sea salt on top of chocolate (evenly).

10. Place in freezer for 20 minutes or fridge for a few hrs.

11. Once they are hardened, remove from fridge.

12. Slice into bars and wrap each one in foil for a quick grab and go bar. Or store in an airtight container.

13. Best kept in fridge for freshness. Feel free to freezer for up to 8-10 weeks. These really do keep well!

Notes

• If your batter is not sticking to the pan after mixing, remove from pan and place in a bowl, mix in a tbs of honey or maple syrup if needed. If the batter is too sticky, add in 1 tbsp of coconut flour.

• An 8×8 pan or 9×13 will work. Your bars will be thinner with 9×13.

• Figs – depending on the type of dried fig you use, you made need to use more than 5oz to get it "sticky" in the batter.

• Chocolate -Use as much or as little as you'd like to on top. The less you use, the thinner the layer of chocolate and vice versa.

Easy & Healthy Avocado Chicken Salad

Use it to complement salad greens or in a sandwich, this Carolina Charm recipe is sure to become a staple in your recipe box.

Ingredients:

• 1 large chicken breast

• salt and pepper

• olive oil

• 1 ripe avocado

• 1 apple

- 1/2 cup celery
- 1/4 cup red onion
- 2 tbsp finely chopped cilantro
- 2 tsp lime juice

Directions:

1. Butterfly your chicken by laying the cutlet flat and slicing it parallel with a knife. Season with salt and pepper. Place the chicken breastsinto a lightly oiled skillet over medium-high heat. Cook until brown and opaque throughout, 2-4 minutes each side. Remove from heat and set aside for a few minutes. Finely dice the chicken breast and toss into a large bowl.

2. Dice your veggies. Wash, dry, peel and finely dice your red onion, apple, celery and avocado. Toss into bowl with chicken. Gently mash the avocado until all of the ingredients are mixed well.

3. Sprinkle in cilantro. Add in lime juice and salt and pepper to taste.

4. Serve as a sandwich or on a bed of greens with a little drizzle of olive oil!

Vegetarian Minestrone Soup

An easy to prepare soup, excellent for chilly days!

Ingredients:

- 1 tbsp extra virgin olive oil
- 3/4 cup chopped onion
- 3 cups water
- 2 cups diced zucchini
- 1 cup peeled and sliced carrots
- 1 cup cannellini beans
- 3/4 cup diced celery
- 2 tbsp finely chopped basil (or 1 tsp dried basil)
- 1/4 tsp dried oregano
- 1/4 tsp salt
- 1/8 tsp freshly ground black pepper
- 28 ounce can of diced plum tomatoes
- 2 cloves garlic, minced

- 1/4 cup uncooked pasta of your choice (ditalini or elbow work great!)

Directions:

1. Heat a large saucepan over medium-high heat.

2. Add oil and onion and saute, stirring occasionally, until lightly browned, about 4 minutes.

3. Add all remaining ingredients to the pan except the pasta and bring to a boil.

4. Reduce heat and simmer covered pan on low heat for 25 minutes, stirring occasionally.

5. Add pasta and cook according to package directions until past a is al dente (approximately 10-12 minutes).

Watermelon, Pineapple, Turmeric Smoothie

Usually thought to only flavor savory dishes, turmeric's great spice and wonderful anti-inflammatory properties are a great addition to sweet treats as well!

Ingredients:

- 2 cups frozen watermelon, cubed

- 2 cups fresh frozen pineapple, cubed

- 1 orange, peeled, seeds removed

- 1/2 cup coconut milk

- 1 1/2 cups coconut water, frozen into cubes

- 1 teaspoon fresh ginger, grated

- 2 teaspoons freshly grated turmeric or 1/2 teaspoon organic turmeric powder

- 2-3 drops of liquid stevia or 1 teaspoon honey (optional)

Directions:

1. Place all ingredients into a blender and blend until smooth.

2. Add optional sweetener to taste, blend, and serve.

Ginger Lemonade

This Ginger Lemonade is a great way to start your day and is delicious enough for company. This drink is rich in vitamin c and antioxidants, and ginger is known for its powerful anti-inflammatory effects.

Ingredients:

- 1/3 cup honey

- 2 tablespoons fresh ginger root, peeled and grated

- 4 large strips of lemon peel

- 2 medium sprigs fresh rosemary

- Juice of 4 lemons

- Lemon slices (for garnish, optional)

- 1 large sprig fresh rosemary (for garnish, optional)

- Ice, for serving

Directions:

1. Combine the honey, ginger, lemon peel and 2 sprigs rosemary in a small pot with 2 cups of water.

2. Bring mixture to a boil, reduce heat and simmer, stirring constantly, for 10 minutes.

3. Remove from heat and let cool, approximately 15 minutes.

4. Once cool, strain mixture into large pitcher. Discard the ginger and rosemary that was left behind in the strainer.

5. To pitcher, add 6 cups cold water and lemon juice. Stir to combine.

6. Serve over ice with small piece of fresh rosemary and lemon slice as garnish (optional).

CONCLUSION

If you are yet to be convinced of the health benefits of doing what your mum always urged and eating your greens, here's one more reason to munch down beans, spinach, brussel sprouts and more green vegetables: tests have shown that broccoli helps to prevent the build-up of fat in the liver. Eating any greens can help you lose weight, which in turn will help your liver. It gives you early satiety (filling of fullness) and is low in calories. Its fibre-rich content can help you lower your blood cholesterol levels.

Ironically, eating fatty fish helps combat a fatty liver. Salmon, sardines, tuna, and trout are all high in omega-3 fatty acids, which can help lower the levels of fat in the liver and can bring down inflammation. It is also a healthy alternative to meat as it gives you the opportunity to avoid consuming the fats and skins from meat or poultry.

If you are not a keen fish eater, you can still get your omega-3 fatty acids from walnuts. They are great to eat as a healthy snack, add to your stir fry for that extra texture or sprinkle over your favourite salad. Limit portion to a small handful per day.

When you need to control your weight and lower liver enzyme levels, you can't go wrong by reducing the amount of fat/oil in your diet. When choosing fat/oil, opt for healthier unsaturated type. Flaxseed oil is an example of unsaturated oil. It is a good source of omega-3 fatty acids. You can dash over a salad, drizzled over bread or used for light frying adds a distinct flavour to all your dishes without you feeling guilty for the indulgence.

Now we are starting to see a pattern. Here's another delicious food choice that's high in healthy fat, yet great for heart and liver health. Avocado appears to contain chemicals that might slow liver damage. Spread a small amount over toast with lemon juice and black pepper, add to a sandwich or wrap, or get really adventurous with the many recipes relating it you can find in this book.

Printed in Great Britain
by Amazon